The cat

that moved to Spain

My name is Kaiser Otto. This is my story.

Acknowle...

My speci...
(as well...
perfec...
for b...

Als...
th...

...dgements

...l thanks go to my "dad", Hans, for helping me tell my story
...as hold the pen!); to Hilary McKnight and Maurice Leitch for
...ing my English; and to my publishers, Alan & Gertrud Roberts,
...lieving in me and my writing skills.

...o, to my "mum", Annika, who actually thinks that she has written
...is book. Cheek!

And, finally, to my new friends, the "campo cats", without whom there
would have been no story to tell.

Kaiser Otto

The cat that moved to Spain

Published by Ediciones Santana, S.L.
Apartado 41
29650 Mijas-Pueblo (Málaga)
Spain

Tel: (0034) 952 48 58 38 Fax: (0034) 952 48 53 67
E-Mail: info@santanabooks.com

Printed in Spain by Grafisur

ISBN: 978-84-89954-68-7

Depósito Legal: CA-716/07

"The more I see of men, the more I like cats."
Mark Twain (well, almost!)

I really have to apologise for the quality of some of the pictures in this book. Especially those taken while I was still living in London. They don't do me justice at all.

My "mum" took them and her excuse is that she used her old camera and — listen to this — she didn't know that I was working on a book about my life. She said: " You are just a cat. Cats cannot write books."

That really made me angry, so I replied: " You are just a human. Humans cannot write books about cats. What do you know about our life, our feelings or anything else that's going on in our world? Nothing! NIL! NADA!"

She just shook her head and sighed as if I was not somebody to be taken seriously. And that upset me even more. I was absolutely determined to write my book. And use some of the bad pictures, just to show her.

And now, you who are reading this book, you can see for yourself. You have the proof in your hands. Couldn't be clearer, could it? So my advice to you humans is: don't be so superior. Show some respect. You are not the only ones contributing good things to this world. On the contrary, thinking about it, you are in fact the guys who are slowly destroying the planet, aren't you? Yes, it's you lot, not us!

Anyway, welcome to my world. And to my adventures.

My name is Kaiser.
It's a grand name. It means Emperor.
Not just simply King or Queen,
but EMPEROR.
I like it. It suits me because,
in my opinion, I'm the best-looking
guy in the whole neighbourhood.

London 1995

I was born in London in 1995. I lived with my first family for about four years. I think so anyway, I'm not very good at figures. That's about the only thing I'm not very good at. Anyway, at that time a Swedish couple moved in next door. There were only the two of them. No kids, no dogs, no other cats. Thank God! So I thought, hmmmm… maybe it's time for a change. I had a long and serious talk with my best friend. His name was Kami. He was much older and wiser than me, so I always asked him for advice on important issues.

I told him about the Swedes and we both went over to have a look. It didn't take long for us to make up our minds. It looked very promising. So, on a Monday afternoon we were ready. We both walked over to their flat and sneaked in through the garden door which was open. And guess what happened?

Tuna on a plate! They had seen us coming! It only took a couple of minutes. I knew it. I looked at Kami and we nodded to each other. Yes, this was definitely the right move. Definitely!

Now for some reason our new mum and dad didn't call us by our real names. No, no, they had to have their own names. So Kami was called The Pirate (because he had only one eye). And I was called Otto for a reason I just cannot grasp. I was a little annoyed, to tell you the truth. I mean, you cannot call an emperor Otto, can you? Then I learned that Otto was the name of a very famous emperor in Europe. And he was very good-looking and very friendly. Just like me. So I accepted being called Otto. Kami said that it didn't matter what they called you as long as they served tuna on a plate. And of course, as usual, he was right.

After about two years my dear friend Kami (OK then, The Pirate) had a very serious heart attack. I have to give our new folks credit. They saved his life. He lived for another two happy years. He died of old age. I think he was at least 18 when he died. I missed him terribly to start with, but then I slowly realised that it was now my turn to be the oldest and wisest. Oh, boy, did I like that.

We moved hundreds of times in London. At least that's what it felt like. Those crazy Swedes always had a new project going on. No consideration for me at all. All those building works, all the noise and all the strange people who arrived early in the morning. It drove me bonkers. So when my folks told me that now we were moving to Spain I thought, they must be joking. SPAIN! Where on earth is that!

Blackmail tricks

I had then lived with those Swedes for about eight years. Time really does fly. And I must say I enjoyed it most of the time. They really love cats, so I can easily trick them into doing anything for me. But if you aren't sure what kind of people you are moving in with, test them with a couple of simple tricks.

So these are my tips to all my cat friends — my best "blackmail tricks".

Limping

This is a funny one. Try this just to keep them on their toes. Limp around the house on three legs. Look miserable. As always they will try everything. Give you nice food (tuna on a plate), mess around with you, put you in their bed, and so on. But here is a lesson to learn. I slightly overdid the trick once. So they took me to the vet. That really put me in an awkward situation. I don't like vets. They give you injections and cut your precious claws. To avoid that I came out of my cage and walked around normally. They were totally confused. But that trick doesn't work any more. They are not that stupid.

Sulking

Pretend to be depressed. Don't react to anything. If they try to pat you, just walk away. If you need to go on like this for more than three hours before they prepare a special treat, then maybe you should think of moving elsewhere.

But, if the people you move in with are upset every time you play a trick, then you have hit the jackpot. Be happy.

Hide and seek

Probably the best trick of all.

Stay away for a day or only a couple of hours. Pretend to be lost. It's worth doing just to see how nervous and upset they are when you suddenly arrive back.

(Most of the time when I do this, I hide very close so that I can see them running around looking for me.)

"Oh, darling Otto, where have you been? We have been looking all over for you. We thought something terrible might have happened to you. But now you're back, we are so happy," they say, in that kind of baby-talk they use with me. Like I'm some kind of an imbecile!

Every time I return after one of those "hide-and-seek" things they behave in the same way. They just never learn. They treat you to the best food possible, you can sleep in their bed and, best of all, even if your paws are really dirty you can jump up on your mum's knee when she's got white trousers on.

Now, as I mentioned before, I have been moving around a lot here in London with these two guys, at least six or seven times. And now they are going to this place called Spain. And they are very serious about it. And you know what: IT'S ABROAD, IT'S IN EUROPE SOMEWHERE!!! I really, really like living in London. I have been here all my life. I like to go with my folks when they are shopping. My favourite place is definitely Harrods. The fish counter at that place makes a cat think he's in heaven. I don't think they have anything like that in this place they call Spain.

And all my cat friends are very sophisticated, just like me. We are used to living in a big city, and my folks are going to the countryside. They say that they are tired of all the noise, all the cars and all the crimes in London. And there are other things as well. In my garden, for example, there is a small house my mum calls her studio. Anyway I used to spend a couple of hours on the roof, teasing the neighbour's dog. He's actually my friend, but I like to tease him. His name is Rocket and he is a whippet but, and it's a shame, he's only got three legs. Another of my friends is Frank the Cat. He's called Frank because he's got blue eyes. It's great fun rambling around in my garden and in the neighbourhood. I also have my own cat-flap. No, not a normal cat-flap, this works with a magnet that I have in my collar, so only I can go in and out as I want. So when my folks started talking about this Spain I decided to do everything in my power to stop that move. I started with my "hide and seek", but they got so upset every time that I felt for them and gave that one up. I went for plan B.

I pretended to be depressed. Didn't work. I started limping but they had no time for that old trick either. Anyway I did everything I could think of to stop this farce.

Then my dad took me in his lap and told me about Spain. He said it was warm all year round. That I was going to get the same food that I'm used to. That I'm even going to get my own mountain to ramble on. A mountain!! Never heard that word before. Well, thinking of it, they call the slopes where you go skiing a mountain, don't they? But there's snow, and we are going to the sun! I'm confused.

I thought I would help with the packing...

As I told you before, my folks are from Sweden, where, I understand it can be really, really cold. Not only minus zero, but very, very minus. But they have snow. I have always wanted to play in the snow. I have seen it on TV and it looks like great fun. I have asked my mum hundreds of times if we could go north to go skiing and she PROMISED that one day we'd go. I was so looking forward to it. I just know I will be a master on the slopes. I can see myself on my special made skis and boots. I have already decided to buy the latest outfit. I definitely have to look cool. Then I only have to put on my specially made goggles, turn on my iPod and off I go.

So what happened to that promise? WE ARE GOING TO SPAIN. My dad is telling me not to worry. Not far away from where I'm going to live there is a ski resort called SIERRA NEVADA. And one day we will go. Another of his promises? We will see.

Anyway, I gave in, but they could have asked me first. That would have been much easier. I would have agreed immediately, because now I'm quite keen to go to Spain, wherever it is. Who wouldn't be?

I mean London is not exactly known for its good weather. It can be cold, and it's very wet. And I really hate cold weather. Yes, I know I have a fur but that doesn't protect me from the rain, does it?

So this is my last Christmas in London. And now, when we all agreed that Spain is going to be great, I thought I would help them with the packing. I told them if they took care of their stuff, I would take care of mine. It took me about three minutes!

We are moving!

It's the third of January 2006 and we are on our way. My mum has bought three one-way tickets. From Gatwick to Málaga. We are all very excited. My ticket cost three times as much as theirs. But, as I say, it costs to travel in style. I had to be at the airport three hours before departure! Some people there had to go through my papers. Proof of my rabies vaccination. Proof that I'm healthy enough to fly. Proof that ME, THE KAISER, is free from fleas!! They even scanned my cage for a bomb! I told them, of course I don't have a bomb with me. I'm not a suicidal cat, am I? But they just wouldn't listen. I felt very insulted. How dare they question me. Me, THE KAISER!

This, by the way, is my passport. I like it because it means that I can travel all over Europe if it happens that I find some other nice people. And you must agree I look quite handsome, even at my age. My folks were all over the place. Their nerves, I suppose. While we were waiting for boarding, I overheard them saying: "It feels really good to be out of the rat-race at last." Out of the rat-race? Don't they realise that's the only race I'm interested in. But, as usual they don't think before they talk.

The flight down was quite ok. They put me in my cage and gave me food and water. For this trip I had ordered some nice salmon mousse as a starter, tender sirloin pieces with veg for main and a mature Cheddar for dessert. I really love mature cheddar, I hope they have it in Spain. I have to give the airline credit, I got everything I had asked for. The one thing that did irritate me was my company. It was a silly-looking little dog who looked like he was going to have a nervous breakdown any second. So after I finished my meal I just dozed off and when I woke up there they were, both of them, harping on at me with their baby-talk. It's a little bit embarrassing when other cats are there, but I know that they just do it to be kind.

The first morning I woke up in Spain was a pleasant surprise. When we left London it was really cold, but here the sun was shining and it was warm. You know, if you are English, moving to Spain is like crawling out from under a wet blanket.
Just around the corner from our little garden there was a huge swimming pool. Not that I'm much for swimming, but it's a great place just to hang out. I can sit there, relax and look gorgeous. And I tell you, I have already seen a couple of chicks here. To tell you the truth, I have already got a new girlfriend. She absolutely adores me.
I'm starting to feel quite good about the whole thing.

We are living in La Carihuela on the Costa del Sol. It's a small place by the sea. My folks very often go down to the beach for a swim. So they say anyway. I think they are just going to the bar for a couple of drinks. I can smell it when they come back. And they just leave me. Never ask me to join them.

NEVER!

I'm a little upset again.

They promised me my own mountain and look what I got. Ok, the sun is shining, but no mountain in sight. The only thing I can see is a big boring wall. And when they are having a good time, what can I do? I cannot sit by the pool all day and chatter with the girls. By the way, I'm getting a little bored by my fiancée as well. She is quite good-looking, but I'm afraid she is a little stupid. She only talks about her looks and what hair shampoo she's using. She even went all the way to Marbella to have her highlights done. I mean, give me a break! So what can I do. I'll tell you. I have started to take some walks in the village. In secret.

So the other day I went off to the beach. Do you think my folks were there? Of course not. I found them at the bar. I have heard them talking about that bar before. It's called Makanaky and they say it's their favourite place in the world. A bit over the top if you ask me.

They are just sitting there drinking and looking at the sea. What kind of life is that? I mean sitting there hour after hour, getting drunk and staring at the sea. Humans are indeed strange. On my first walk I got an unpleasant surprise. The Spaniards have an irritating habit of keeping canaries and other small, tasty birds in cages. Those birds are untouchable. I see them everywhere, sitting there and singing, having a good time. It drives me crazy. It's torture, thinking of the joy of catching them. I can just imagine the taste. As you know by now, humans are not my favourite species, but some of them — the bird-lovers — got one thing right. I support them wholeheartedly when they say that wild birds should be just that, wild. Sometimes I go to the local fishmonger. He's a very fine man, he always give me bits of fish when I am passing by. And at the back of the butcher's shop you can always find a treat. Not that I need anything, my folks give me anything I want, but that's where all the other cats in La Carihuela are coming together. So I join them from time to time. Just to listen to the latest gossip.

I must say that the Spanish people are very nice and polite, not at all what I had expected.

It's now the 25th of March. I have been living in La Carihuela for almost three months.And just when I am starting to feel at home – I even have a plan worked out how to catch the canaries – guess what has happened.

I cannot believe it.

We are moving again!!

This time to a place called Mijas Pueblo. It's up somewhere in that thing they call the mountain. I am getting too old and tired for this.

PLEASE!

HERE I AM.

Okay, I have to give them some credit. I got myself a garden. There is even some shade in it, because, oh boy, is it hot here! My folks seem to like it as well. Maybe this is it. No more moving. That would suit me perfectly. I can live with this.

On the other hand, they did promise me my own mountain. Remember? You see that thing over there? That's a mountain. I wonder which one is mine. But, hang on, those mountains are miles away. I cannot get there, can I? **TYPICAL!**

Well, well, what can I say?
You don't have this view anywhere in London. Not even from Big Ben. And I like sitting on the wall, looking down on the other cats. That suits me perfectly. That's one reason I like this place. The other is that my dad suffers from very severe vertigo. So when I'm sitting on the fence, he gets sick. Almost. That's my revenge for the loss of the mountain. And the skiing!

Did you really think I was going to have MY garden to MYSELF?

No way. I've suddenly realised that there are quite a lot of cats in the neighbourhood. They come in all colours and sizes. And they are camping in MY garden!

I really made an effort to socialise in the beginning. And I have to tell you that wasn't easy. I mean, after all, I'm a sophisticated cat from London and those guys are from Spain. And not even from a town, but a small village in the middle of nowhere. We don't have much in common, if you know what I mean. What do they know about real life? NADA!

They even try to steal my food. And my toys. And they come to drink as well, even if I think they are mostly used to cheap red vino. So a nice Pinot Noir from France is a waste on them. The same goes for a Dry Martini. Those guys have probably not even seen a glass before. It's lucky my friends in London cannot see my new compadres!

The Tiger

This guy was the only one I could call a friend. I called him The Tiger and he reminded me a lot of The Pirate. He was the boss of the "campo cats" (that's Spanglish for uneducated, uncivilised, stupid cats from the countryside). That's precisely why we got on so well. We were very much alike. We had the same dignified attitude to life, we were both born to be leaders.

Sadly I have to inform you that The Tiger is not around any more. We have a neighbour who is really nasty. He doesn't like cats. But, certainly, there was no reason to behave the way he did. I must admit that I'm not so keen on all those cats either, but I would never wish them dead. Never in my life.

When we moved here there were many cats around. I heard they have been here for donkey's years. They have no home as such, no, their home is here. On this little street they have been fed by a lovely old Spanish woman, and no one saw any reason to interfere with their life. My folk wanted to help the old lady to feed the cats, so they did. I had no objection really (AS IF THEY BOTHERED TO ASK). I mean, I always get my food inside, come rain or shine. But in the end we are all cats, so some kind of camaraderie would be appropriate, I suppose.

This man who lives further down the street doesn't like cats at all. So what did he do? He called the town hall, probably stating that all those cats were a health issue or something. Suddenly this man from the council turned up with a big cage. I don't want to go into details, but it wasn't pretty. And it went on for a long time. In the end this cruel man managed to "get rid" of 15 cats. Two were mothers with small kittens. My folks had several heated arguments with the man. I have, once again, to give them credit. They really stood up for us cats. It went so far that they reported him to the police. We are still waiting for the case to go to court. I will keep you posted.

Yes, I do miss The Tiger. Why did they have to take him away? He was quite old, he didn't bother anyone and everyone looked up to him.

All these guys applied to my folks for asylum, claiming they had been subject to murder, torture and discrimination. All of them! And, of course, my folks granted them all asylum as refugees. Without question. How naive can one be. I mean, everyone knows that most so-called refugees are economic refugees. That's common knowledge. So I thought my folks should be a little more suspicious. Ask a few questions. Do you think they listened to me? After all, I'm the one who has to share my food with them!!

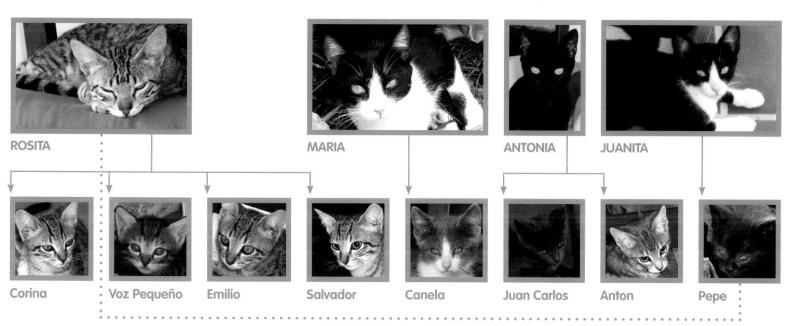

ROSITA   MARIA   ANTONIA   JUANITA

Corina   Voz Pequeño   Emilio   Salvador   Canela   Juan Carlos   Anton   Pepe

This is my mum. See what she's doing. Fiddling around with those stupid cats like she was 10 years old. And what about me? What about a little solidarity? I mean, I didn't protest when they dragged me down here. I am certainly not prepared to share my life with a bunch of stupid "campo cats". I'm an old guy, not that old, mind you, but old enough not to get excited playing with a water hose. She wants me to do it, says it would do me good to be friends with the "campos". Well, that's what she says, but I know it has nothing to do with that. No, she just has a bad conscience because they haven't given ME what they promised. No mountain, no skiing, not even my own GARDEN!! So you can see for yourself what I'm confronted with. PHEW!!

It's not only my mum who is playing with the "campos". Here, our nice neighbour from upstairs is doing the same thing. So you can see my problem.

Trouble started in July. Suddenly these two turned up. All right, I thought, I can live with this. Little did I know what was coming!

IT WAS THE START OF AN INVASION.

Look! Here are three more.

So tell me if I'm wrong. Who needs enemies when you have "friends" like this? I have only one thing to say:

I DON'T DO SHARING!!

Hey, do I have a say at all?
This guy, Mr Kaiser – yes, that's what I have to call him – is an arrogant sod. A bleeding Londoner, a city cat, who comes down here thinking he is better than the rest of us. And knows everything about everything. I have met them before and I hate them.

I heard that.
Don't dare come into my garden and criticise ME.
Just look at this! As far away from a cute kitten as you can get. You "campo cats" have absolutely no manners at all, that's what I think.

Disgusting!

I can't cope with this. Enough is enough. I have to find a plan B.

UNPROBLEMA GRANDE.

This is where I intend to spend my time from now on, which will give my folks something to think about.

Unfortunately it turned out to be easier said than done.

Can you believe this! A "campo dog" on top of everything else! God give me strength.

From time to time I pop into my garden to see if they are still there. Boy oh boy! They are not just there, there seem to be even more of those stupid "campo cats". And on top of that, they seem to have settled in.

And worst of all. They start looking really cute as well.
Flirting with my mum. Trying all sorts of tricks.

All for one purpose alone. They want to

STAY FOREVER!

After all, this place is heaven for a cat.

Why do you think there is a catflap? Brainy!

Why is it that cats from the countryside are so stupid??
I don't know, and I honestly don't care. But what I do know is that my friends from London would suss this thing out in a second, naturally.

Look!
I mean, what on earth is she
doing????
There is nothing there.

NOTHING, STUPID!

Hey, you there! Nobody talks to me in that tone. Nobody!
This is not London. No, this is Mijas Pueblo and here we have all
kinds of things to chase. And if you must know, I have a gecko in
sight. But you probably don't know what that is, do you? I must
say, Kaiser – I refuse to call you Mister – you have a lot to learn.

Thinking about it, I have actually had enough of your egoism. You just don't understand how lucky you are. The only thing you do, if you ask me, is complain. You are a spoiled brat. All my friends here have had a rough start in life. Why don't you listen to their stories for a change? Or, if not, can you at least please shut up, because I am trying to have my siesta.

As if having to deal with those cats wasn't enough, now they are telling me what to do as well. And telling me their boring life stories.

For God's sake, give me a break!

Now Mr Kaiser, can I tell my story please?

I don't know where I was born, but I ended up here in your garden when I was about three weeks old, together with my stunning sister. As you can see, I wasn't feeling too well. Unfortunately my sister, I called her The Angel, died after about two weeks. I missed her a lot. She was my best, and only, friend. So it was only me and my mother now. Then after about another two weeks, my mother disappeared. I was absolutely devastated. No mother, no food. I looked everywhere for her. I called for her but to no avail. I felt that I was the loneliest kitten in the whole wide world.

Now I know what happened. It was your neighbour who took her away from me. What was he thinking, that cruel man? What about me?

I was desperate. But, luckily for me, some other kittens noticed my despair and took me in. It felt so good. And after a while, their fantastic mother accepted me too. I was adopted! And since that day we are friends for ever. Ever and ever.

Life was wonderful. A new mother and four new sisters and brothers. I had a lovely garden to play in, and I had your mum and dad as well looking after me. It was only you, Mr Kaiser, that didn't like me. That hurt!

Everything was fine until one day your mum and dad gave me away to some other people in the pueblo. I think I was about five months old. They said that they couldn't take care of so many cats. Imagine that, Mr Kaiser, suddenly you are being taken to people you have never seen before. I bet you wouldn't like that.

I didn't like it either. So, for four days I did nothing but cry. And, thank god, it worked. Your mum and dad took me back and I was really welcomed home. So now I have a fantastic life. But I have to tell you, Mr Kaiser, I have had to fight for it.

Please, please, Mr Kaiser, why can't you be a little more understanding? I've just lost my mother. I have no one else. I have been looking for her everywhere, but I can't find her. I don't know, but now when I've heard about the horrible neighbour I think maybe the worst has happened. I tell you, Mr Kaiser, it is not easy to find food or water. Please understand. Since I've come here I have both food and water and friends to take care of me.

You probably haven't noticed, but we have had a few cats here that have been very, very ill. If it hadn't been for your lovely folks I would have been dead by now. I still don't know what was wrong, but it might have been poison. There were four of us who suddenly got very sick. Two of my friends, unfortunately, died. But I and Voz Pequeño made it. I don't know how many times I've been to the vet now. It feels like hundreds. I've had at least 10 injections, a blood test, an X-ray and a cancer test. Your folks even took me home when I needed a drip. You should have seen it when your dad carried the cage and your mum held the dripbag, walking through the pueblo. Everybody was looking. Even though I was very sick at that moment, I felt really special.

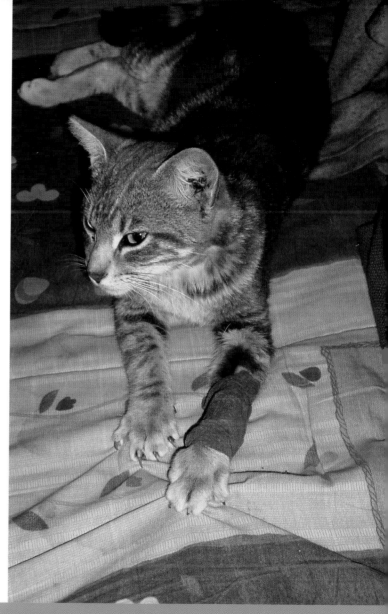

So, as you can see, Mr Kaiser, we have to stick together. And we always do. We actually had a vote yesterday about letting you in, because I think that we ALL should stick together, but, unfortunately, it was only me who voted yes. The others didn't think you were qualified. So I guess you just have to wait.

You can stick together as much as you like. Just count me out. You can have the garden, and all your "nature" to yourself, as well. No, I'm sticking to my friends on the street. When the sun has set and the stupid dog is inside, I and my friend here often go for a ride. It's really cool. I don't know any other cat who has a bike like this.

And when I'm not out with my friends I'm mostly inside. There's nothing you can do about that. You lot are not allowed inside, are you? This is MY HOME and I can tell you it's cosy and warm in here.

I never thought I would say this about my dad but he is a traitor. That's what he is. He used to be an intelligent and very clever guy. And now? He is in the hands of the "campos".

This is my dad.

Having said that, I have recently noticed that something odd is going on in the kitchen.

My dad often says to my mum that she is too soft on the cats. That life revolves too much around the cats. I couldn't agree more.

But do you know what I've seen?

When my mum can't see it, my dad closes the door to the kitchen and opens the window for the cats! Yep, I have seen it many times. And he gives them food. Sometimes they eat from MY BOWL!

What next? Are the "campos" taking over on the inside as well?

una gata de raza

Okay, back to the street. And back to my new girlfriend. What do you think? Not bad, eh! She's *una gata de raza*. If you "campos" know what that means. She absolutely adores me, and loves to listen to my stories from London. She says she wants to go there with me, but, unfortunately, she's got no passport.

This particular girl lives around the corner from my house. She always flirts and tries to talk to me when I'm walking by. She's OK looking, but I don't like her that much. I think she's a dope-head. She is definitely not *una gata de raza*. And she is a big problem.

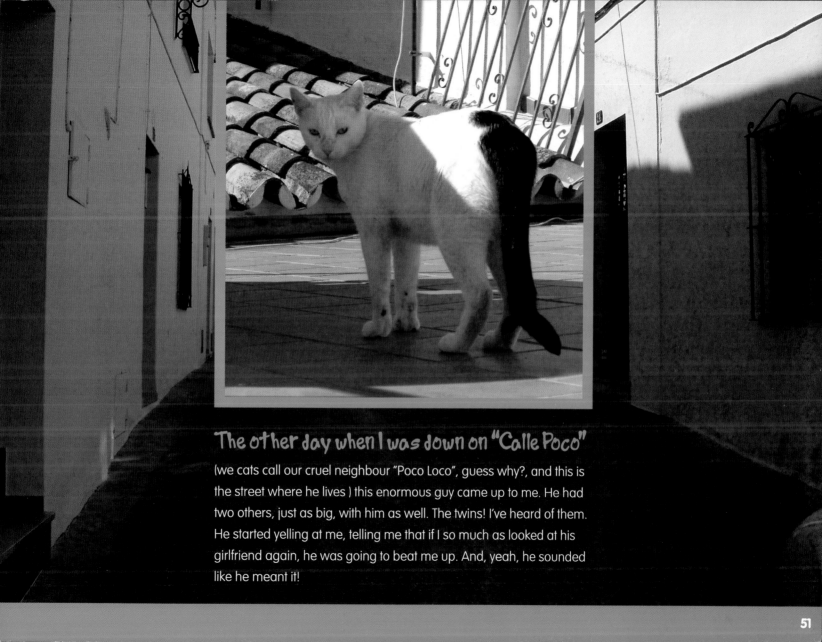

The other day when I was down on "Calle Poco"

(we cats call our cruel neighbour "Poco Loco", guess why?, and this is the street where he lives) this enormous guy came up to me. He had two others, just as big, with him as well. The twins! I've heard of them. He started yelling at me, telling me that if I so much as looked at his girlfriend again, he was going to beat me up. And, yeah, he sounded like he meant it!

" What girlfriend?" I said.

"Don't be stupid!" he yelled. *"You know her very well. You walk by her window almost every day. If you don't stop doing that, you will be dead meat."* Jeepers, I thought. Dope-head!

"Take it easy now, my good man," I said. "Let's sort this little misunderstanding out in a civilised way."

"You can take your 'civilised way' and run to Venezuela. One more word out of you and you are dead."

"Yeah, run!" said one of his stupid bodyguards.

"To Venezuela!" the other said.

So what now, I thought. These guys mean business. That's when I heard it. Down the road they came. All of them. Rosita, María, Antonia, Juanita, Corina, Voz Pequena, Emilio, Salvador, Canela, Juan Carlos, Antón and Pepe. Wow, was I glad to see them. They stopped and Rosita said, in a very quiet voice:

"You stupid. You are just a terrorist. Don't talk to Mr Kaiser, our dear friend, in such a manner. Now this is your choice. Run as far and long as you can, and then a bit more, because if not..."

That was enough. First one of the bodyguards ran off, Voz Pequeña chasing him just for fun. Then the other did the same.

Only the big guy, "Señor Fiancée", was left.

"OK," I said to my new friends. "Let's give the guy a chance." And I turned to him and said: "Leave this pueblo. It ain't big enough for both of us!"

I heard the "campos" sigh behind me.

"He is doing it again," Anton said.

"They are like that, those Londoners," Rosita said. "They just have to be *macho*."

"Señor Fiancée" was far gone by then. And hopefully we will never see him again.

This was the time when everything around me changed. From now on, I had seven new friends. My best friends ever. I have stopped calling them "stupid campo cats". I call them by their proper names now. They have asked me if they can call me Kaiser, not Mr Kaiser. But that, I think, is to stretch it a bit too far. Mr Kaiser will do fine for now, thank you very much.

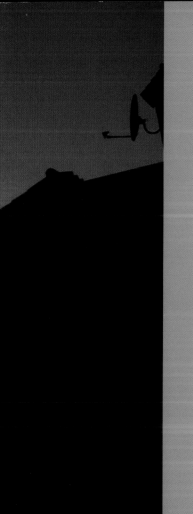

Now you have come to the end of my book.
A lot of talk, and a lot of time spent on everyone but me!
I have only lived in Spain for one year! Who knows how this adventure
is going to end! But for now, thank you very much for listening. It has
been a pleasure.

Lots of love, and see you soon.

KAISER OTTO

I cannot believe this. Just when I finished my book and I thought that everything was more or less under control this little kitten turned up. And, yes, he came with five sisters and brothers! Don't tell me it's starting all over again!